GOOD Night

GOD

A Bedtime
PRAYER MAP
for Kids

BARBOUR **kidz**
A Division of Barbour Publishing

Published by Barbour Publishing, Inc., 1810 Barbour Drive, Uhrichsville, Ohio 44683, www.barbourbooks.com

Our mission is to inspire the world with the life-changing message of the Bible.

Member of the
Evangelical Christian
Publishers Association

Printed in China.

001350 0922 DS

What Do "Good Night" Prayers Look Like?...

Every night is better when you take time to tell God, "Good night!" See for yourself with this fun journal. . . where every colorful page will help you create your very own prayer map—as you write out thoughts, ideas, and lists, which you can follow (from start to finish!)— as you talk to God. (Be sure to include the date on each one of your prayer maps so you can look back over time and see how God has worked in your life!)

Good Night, God: A Bedtime Prayer Map will encourage you to spend time talking with God about ALL the things: the things you're worried about. . .the things you're happy about. . .the things you're sad about. . .the things you're excited about. . . Because God cares about *YOU* most of all!

Date: _____

Dear God,

Today was:
- ☐ GOOD
- ☐ VERY GOOD
- ☐ BAD
- ☐ VERY BAD
- ☐ _____

(Fill in the blank)

Right now I am:
- ☐ HAPPY
- ☐ WORRIED
- ☐ SAD
- ☐ MAD
- ☐ _____

(Fill in the blank)

With You in my life, God, every day can be a VERY GOOD day!

It's important to look for good things every day. Here's a list of good things that happened today:

....
....
....
....
....
....
....

God, thank You for good things!

God, You give me blessings—BIG and small—every day.
Here's a list of all the blessings I noticed today:

....

....

....

....

God, thank You for blessings!

God, I want You to know. . .

....

....

....

....

....

....

Please help me make tomorrow
a VERY GOOD day! Amen.
GOOD NIGHT, GOD!

*Learn to pray about everything. Give thanks
to God as you ask Him for what you need.*
PHILIPPIANS 4:6

Date:

Dear God,

Today was:

☐ GOOD
☐ VERY GOOD
☐ BAD
☐ VERY BAD
☐ _____
(Fill in the blank)

Right now I am:

☐ HAPPY
☐ WORRIED
☐ SAD
☐ MAD
☐ _____
(Fill in the blank)

With You in my life, God, every day can be a VERY GOOD day!

It's important to look for good things every day. Here's a list of good things that happened today:

....

....

....

....

....

....

God, thank You for good things!

God, You give me blessings—BIG and small—every day. Here's a list of all the blessings I noticed today:

....

....

....

God, thank You for blessings!

God, I want You to know. . .

....

....

....

....

....

....

Please help me make tomorrow
a VERY GOOD day! Amen.
GOOD NIGHT, GOD!

"I will spread out my hands to the Lord."
EXODUS 9:29

Date:

Dear God,

Today was:
☐ GOOD
☐ VERY GOOD
☐ BAD
☐ VERY BAD
☐ _____
(Fill in the blank)

Right now I am:
☐ HAPPY
☐ WORRIED
☐ SAD
☐ MAD
☐ _____
(Fill in the blank)

With You in my life, God, every day can be a VERY GOOD day!

It's important to look for good things every day. Here's a list of good things that happened today:

God, thank You for good things!

God, You give me blessings—BIG and small—every day. Here's a list of all the blessings I noticed today:

_____

_____

_____

_____

God, thank You for blessings!

God, I want You to know. . .

_____

_____

_____

_____

_____

_____

Please help me make tomorrow
a VERY GOOD day! Amen.
GOOD NIGHT, GOD!

*"Listen to the cry and to the prayer which
Your servant prays to You today."*
1 KINGS 8:28

Dear God,

Today was:

☐ GOOD
☐ VERY GOOD
☐ BAD
☐ VERY BAD
☐ _____
(Fill in the blank)

Right now I am:

☐ HAPPY
☐ WORRIED
☐ SAD
☐ MAD
☐ _____
(Fill in the blank)

With You in my life, God, every day can be a VERY GOOD day!

It's important to look for good things every day. Here's a list of good things that happened today:

....

....

....

....

....

....

God, thank You for good things!

God, You give me blessings—BIG and small—every day.
Here's a list of all the blessings I noticed today:

....

....

....

....

God, thank You for blessings!

God, I want You to know. . .

....

....

....

....

....

....

Please help me make tomorrow
a VERY GOOD day! Amen.
GOOD NIGHT, GOD!

*The Lord will send His loving-kindness in
the day. And His song will be with me in the
night, a prayer to the God of my life.*
PSALM 42:8

Date:

Dear God,

Today was:

☐ GOOD

☐ VERY GOOD

☐ BAD

☐ VERY BAD

☐ _____

(Fill in the blank)

Right now I am:

☐ HAPPY

☐ WORRIED

☐ SAD

☐ MAD

☐ _____

(Fill in the blank)

With You in my life, God, every day can be a VERY GOOD day!

It's important to look for good things every day. Here's a list of good things that happened today:

God, thank You for good things!

God, You give me blessings—BIG and small—every day.
Here's a list of all the blessings I noticed today:

....

....

....

....

God, thank You for blessings!

God, I want You to know. . .

....

....

....

....

....

....

Please help me make tomorrow
a VERY GOOD day! Amen.
GOOD NIGHT, GOD!

*Then God made the two great lights, the brighter
light to rule the day, and the smaller light
to rule the night. He made the stars also.*
GENESIS 1:16

Date: _____

Dear God,

Today was:
- ☐ GOOD
- ☐ VERY GOOD
- ☐ BAD
- ☐ VERY BAD
- ☐ _____
  (Fill in the blank)

Right now I am:
- ☐ HAPPY
- ☐ WORRIED
- ☐ SAD
- ☐ MAD
- ☐ _____
  (Fill in the blank)

With You in my life, God, every day can be a VERY GOOD day!

It's important to look for good things every day. Here's a list of good things that happened today:

....

....

....

....

....

....

God, thank You for good things!

God, You give me blessings—BIG and small—every day.
Here's a list of all the blessings I noticed today:

....

....

....

....

God, thank You for blessings!

God, I want You to know. . .

....

....

....

....

....

....

Please help me make tomorrow
a VERY GOOD day! Amen.
GOOD NIGHT, GOD!

I will lie down and sleep in peace.
O Lord, You alone keep me safe.
PSALM 4:8

Date: _____

Dear God,

Today was:
- ☐ GOOD
- ☐ VERY GOOD
- ☐ BAD
- ☐ VERY BAD
- ☐ _____

(Fill in the blank)

Right now I am:
- ☐ HAPPY
- ☐ WORRIED
- ☐ SAD
- ☐ MAD
- ☐ _____

(Fill in the blank)

With You in my life, God, every day can be a VERY GOOD day!

It's important to look for good things every day. Here's a list of good things that happened today:

....

....

....

....

....

....

God, thank You for good things!

God, You give me blessings—BIG and small—every day.
Here's a list of all the blessings I noticed today:

....

....

....

....

God, thank You for blessings!

God, I want You to know. . .

....

....

....

....

....

....

Please help me make tomorrow
a VERY GOOD day! Amen.
GOOD NIGHT, GOD!

*I will say to the Lord, "You are my safe and
strong place, my God, in Whom I trust."*
PSALM 91:2

Date:

Dear God,

Today was:

☐ GOOD
☐ VERY GOOD
☐ BAD
☐ VERY BAD
☐ _____

(Fill in the blank)

Right now I am:

☐ HAPPY
☐ WORRIED
☐ SAD
☐ MAD
☐ _____

(Fill in the blank)

With You in my life, God, every day can be a VERY GOOD day!

It's important to look for good things every day. Here's a list of good things that happened today:

....

....

....

....

....

....

....

God, thank You for good things!

God, You give me blessings—BIG and small—every day. Here's a list of all the blessings I noticed today:

....

....

....

God, thank You for blessings!

God, I want You to know. . .

....

....

....

....

....

Please help me make tomorrow
a VERY GOOD day! Amen.
GOOD NIGHT, GOD!

*My voice goes up to God
and He will hear me.*
PSALM 77:1

Date: _____

Dear God,

Today was:
☐ GOOD
☐ VERY GOOD
☐ BAD
☐ VERY BAD
☐ _____
(Fill in the blank)

Right now I am:
☐ HAPPY
☐ WORRIED
☐ SAD
☐ MAD
☐ _____
(Fill in the blank)

With You in my life, God, every day can be a VERY GOOD day!

It's important to look for good things every day. Here's a list of good things that happened today:

....
....
....
....
....
....

God, thank You for good things!

God, You give me blessings—BIG and small—every day. Here's a list of all the blessings I noticed today:

....

....

....

....

God, thank You for blessings!

God, I want You to know. . .

....

....

....

....

....

....

Please help me make tomorrow
a VERY GOOD day! Amen.
GOOD NIGHT, GOD!

*The day is Yours. And the night
is Yours. You have set the light
and the sun in their places.*
PSALM 74:16

Date:

Dear God,

Today was:
- [ ] GOOD
- [ ] VERY GOOD
- [ ] BAD
- [ ] VERY BAD
- [ ] _____
  (Fill in the blank)

Right now I am:
- [ ] HAPPY
- [ ] WORRIED
- [ ] SAD
- [ ] MAD
- [ ] _____
  (Fill in the blank)

With You in my life, God, every day can be a VERY GOOD day!

It's important to look for good things every day. Here's a list of good things that happened today:

....

....

....

....

....

....

God, thank You for good things!

God, You give me blessings—BIG and small—every day.
Here's a list of all the blessings I noticed today:

....

....

....

....

God, thank You for blessings!

God, I want You to know. . .

....

....

....

....

....

....

Please help me make tomorrow
a VERY GOOD day! Amen.
GOOD NIGHT, GOD!

*You, O Lord, have helped
me and comforted me.*
PSALM 86:17

Date: _____

Dear God,

Today was:
- ☐ GOOD
- ☐ VERY GOOD
- ☐ BAD
- ☐ VERY BAD
- ☐ _____
  (Fill in the blank)

Right now I am:
- ☐ HAPPY
- ☐ WORRIED
- ☐ SAD
- ☐ MAD
- ☐ _____
  (Fill in the blank)

With You in my life, God, every day can be a VERY GOOD day!

It's important to look for good things every day. Here's a list of good things that happened today:

....

....

....

....

....

....

God, thank You for good things!

God, You give me blessings—BIG and small—every day. Here's a list of all the blessings I noticed today:

....

....

....

....

God, thank You for blessings!

God, I want You to know. . .

....

....

....

....

....

....

Please help me make tomorrow
a VERY GOOD day! Amen.
GOOD NIGHT, GOD!

My soul is quiet and waits for God alone.
PSALM 62:1

Date:

Dear God,

Today was:
- ☐ GOOD
- ☐ VERY GOOD
- ☐ BAD
- ☐ VERY BAD
- ☐ _____
  (Fill in the blank)

Right now I am:
- ☐ HAPPY
- ☐ WORRIED
- ☐ SAD
- ☐ MAD
- ☐ _____
  (Fill in the blank)

With You in my life, God, every day can be a VERY GOOD day!

It's important to look for good things every day. Here's a list of good things that happened today:

....

....

....

....

....

....

....

God, thank You for good things!

God, You give me blessings—BIG and small—every day.
Here's a list of all the blessings I noticed today:

....

....

....

« God, thank You for blessings!

God, I want You to know. . .

....

....

....

....

....

....

Please help me make tomorrow
a VERY GOOD day! Amen.
GOOD NIGHT, GOD!

Hear my prayer, O God.
Listen to the words of my mouth.
PSALM 54:2

Dear God,

Today was:

☐ GOOD
☐ VERY GOOD
☐ BAD
☐ VERY BAD
☐ _____
(Fill in the blank)

Right now I am:

☐ HAPPY
☐ WORRIED
☐ SAD
☐ MAD
☐ _____
(Fill in the blank)

With You in my life, God, every day can be a VERY GOOD day!

It's important to look for good things every day. Here's a list of good things that happened today:

God, thank You for good things!

God, You give me blessings—BIG and small—every day.
Here's a list of all the blessings I noticed today:

....

....

....

....

God, thank You for blessings!

God, I want You to know. . .

....

....

....

....

....

....

Please help me make tomorrow
a VERY GOOD day! Amen.
GOOD NIGHT, GOD!

*When they came out and prayed that
good would come to the people,
the shining-greatness of the Lord
was shown to all the people.*
LEVITICUS 9:23

Date:

Dear God,

Today was:
- ☐ GOOD
- ☐ VERY GOOD
- ☐ BAD
- ☐ VERY BAD
- ☐ _____

(Fill in the blank)

Right now I am:
- ☐ HAPPY
- ☐ WORRIED
- ☐ SAD
- ☐ MAD
- ☐ _____

(Fill in the blank)

With You in my life, God, every day can be a VERY GOOD day!

It's important to look for good things every day. Here's a list of good things that happened today:

....

....

....

....

....

....

....

God, thank You for good things!

God, You give me blessings—BIG and small—every day.
Here's a list of all the blessings I noticed today:

....

....

....

....

God, thank You for blessings!

God, I want You to know. . .

....

....

....

....

....

....

Please help me make tomorrow
a VERY GOOD day! Amen.
GOOD NIGHT, GOD!

> "Now, I pray, let the power
> of the Lord be great."
> NUMBERS 14:17

Date:

Dear God,

Today was:
☐ GOOD
☐ VERY GOOD
☐ BAD
☐ VERY BAD
☐ _____
(Fill in the blank)

Right now I am:
☐ HAPPY
☐ WORRIED
☐ SAD
☐ MAD
☐ _____
(Fill in the blank)

With You in my life, God, every day can be a VERY GOOD day!

It's important to look for good things every day. Here's a list of good things that happened today:

God, thank You for good things!

God, You give me blessings—BIG and small—every day.
Here's a list of all the blessings I noticed today:

....

....

....

....

God, thank You for blessings!

God, I want You to know. . .

....

....

....

....

....

....

Please help me make tomorrow
a VERY GOOD day! Amen.
GOOD NIGHT, GOD!

*O Lord, the God Who saves me, I have
cried out before You day and night.*
PSALM 88:1

Date:

Dear God,

Today was:

☐ GOOD
☐ VERY GOOD
☐ BAD
☐ VERY BAD
☐ _____
(Fill in the blank)

Right now I am:

☐ HAPPY
☐ WORRIED
☐ SAD
☐ MAD
☐ _____
(Fill in the blank)

With You in my life, God, every day can be a VERY GOOD day!

It's important to look for good things every day. Here's a list of good things that happened today:

God, thank You for good things!

God, You give me blessings—BIG and small—every day.
Here's a list of all the blessings I noticed today:

....

....

....

....

God, thank You for blessings!

God, I want You to know. . .

....

....

....

....

....

Please help me make tomorrow
a VERY GOOD day! Amen.
GOOD NIGHT, GOD!

> *But as for me, I will watch for the Lord.*
> *I will wait for the God Who saves*
> *me. My God will hear me.*
> MICAH 7:7

Date: _____

Dear God,

Today was:

☐ GOOD
☐ VERY GOOD
☐ BAD
☐ VERY BAD
☐ _____
(Fill in the blank)

Right now I am:

☐ HAPPY
☐ WORRIED
☐ SAD
☐ MAD
☐ _____
(Fill in the blank)

With You in my life, God, every day can be a VERY GOOD day!

It's important to look for good things every day. Here's a list of good things that happened today:

....

....

....

....

....

....

God, thank You for good things!

God, You give me blessings—BIG and small—every day. Here's a list of all the blessings I noticed today:

....

....

....

....

God, thank You for blessings!

God, I want You to know. . .

....

....

....

....

....

Please help me make tomorrow
a VERY GOOD day! Amen.
GOOD NIGHT, GOD!

"My heart is happy in the Lord."
1 SAMUEL 2:1

Date:

Dear God,

Today was:
- ☐ GOOD
- ☐ VERY GOOD
- ☐ BAD
- ☐ VERY BAD
- ☐ _____
  (Fill in the blank)

Right now I am:
- ☐ HAPPY
- ☐ WORRIED
- ☐ SAD
- ☐ MAD
- ☐ _____
  (Fill in the blank)

With You in my life, God, every day can be a VERY GOOD day!

It's important to look for good things every day. Here's a list of good things that happened today:

God, thank You for good things!

God, You give me blessings—BIG and small—every day. Here's a list of all the blessings I noticed today:

....

....

....

....

God, thank You for blessings!

God, I want You to know. . .

....

....

....

....

....

....

Please help me make tomorrow a VERY GOOD day! Amen.

GOOD NIGHT, GOD!

"Do not worry about tomorrow. Tomorrow will have its own worries. The troubles we have in a day are enough for one day."
MATTHEW 6:34

Date:

Dear God,

Today was:
- ☐ GOOD
- ☐ VERY GOOD
- ☐ BAD
- ☐ VERY BAD
- ☐ _____

(Fill in the blank)

Right now I am:
- ☐ HAPPY
- ☐ WORRIED
- ☐ SAD
- ☐ MAD
- ☐ _____

(Fill in the blank)

With You in my life, God, every day can be a VERY GOOD day!

It's important to look for good things every day. Here's a list of good things that happened today:

God, thank You for good things!

God, You give me blessings—BIG and small—every day.
Here's a list of all the blessings I noticed today:

....

....

....

....

God, thank You for blessings!

God, I want You to know. . .

....

....

....

....

....

....

Please help me make tomorrow
a VERY GOOD day! Amen.
GOOD NIGHT, GOD!

[The Lord] Who watches over you will not sleep.
PSALM 121:3

Date:

Dear God,

Today was:
- ☐ GOOD
- ☐ VERY GOOD
- ☐ BAD
- ☐ VERY BAD
- ☐ _____

(Fill in the blank)

Right now I am:
- ☐ HAPPY
- ☐ WORRIED
- ☐ SAD
- ☐ MAD
- ☐ _____

(Fill in the blank)

With You in my life, God, every day can be a VERY GOOD day!

It's important to look for good things every day. Here's a list of good things that happened today:

God, thank You for good things!

God, You give me blessings—BIG and small—every day. Here's a list of all the blessings I noticed today:

....

....

....

....

God, thank You for blessings!

God, I want You to know. . .

....

....

....

....

....

....

Please help me make tomorrow
a VERY GOOD day! Amen.
GOOD NIGHT, GOD!

> *"The Lord has given me what I asked of Him."*
> 1 SAMUEL 1:27

Date:

Dear God,

Today was:
☐ GOOD
☐ VERY GOOD
☐ BAD
☐ VERY BAD
☐ _____
(Fill in the blank)

Right now I am:
☐ HAPPY
☐ WORRIED
☐ SAD
☐ MAD
☐ _____
(Fill in the blank)

With You in my life, God, every day can be a VERY GOOD day!

It's important to look for good things every day. Here's a list of good things that happened today:

God, thank You for good things!

God, You give me blessings—BIG and small—every day. Here's a list of all the blessings I noticed today:

....

....

....

....

God, thank You for blessings!

God, I want You to know. . .

....

....

....

....

....

....

Please help me make tomorrow a VERY GOOD day! Amen.
GOOD NIGHT, GOD!

*[God] knows the number of the stars.
He gives names to all of them.*
PSALM 147:4

Date:

Dear God,

Today was:
- ☐ GOOD
- ☐ VERY GOOD
- ☐ BAD
- ☐ VERY BAD
- ☐ _____

(Fill in the blank)

Right now I am:
- ☐ HAPPY
- ☐ WORRIED
- ☐ SAD
- ☐ MAD
- ☐ _____

(Fill in the blank)

With You in my life, God, every day can be a VERY GOOD day!

It's important to look for good things every day. Here's a list of good things that happened today:

....

....

....

....

....

....

God, thank You for good things!

God, You give me blessings—BIG and small—every day.
Here's a list of all the blessings I noticed today:

....

....

....

....

God, thank You for blessings!

God, I want You to know. . .

....

....

....

....

....

Please help me make tomorrow
a VERY GOOD day! Amen.
GOOD NIGHT, GOD!

"O Lord the God of Israel. . . You are the God,
and You alone, of all the nations of the earth.
You have made heaven and earth."
2 KINGS 19:15

Date:

Dear God,

Today was:

☐ GOOD
☐ VERY GOOD
☐ BAD
☐ VERY BAD
☐ _____
(Fill in the blank)

Right now I am:

☐ HAPPY
☐ WORRIED
☐ SAD
☐ MAD
☐ _____
(Fill in the blank)

With You in my life, God, every day can be a VERY GOOD day!

It's important to look for good things every day. Here's a list of good things that happened today:

....

....

....

....

....

....

God, thank You for good things!

God, You give me blessings—BIG and small—every day. Here's a list of all the blessings I noticed today:

....

....

....

....

God, thank You for blessings!

God, I want You to know. . .

....

....

....

....

....

....

Please help me make tomorrow
a VERY GOOD day! Amen.
GOOD NIGHT, GOD!

"If My people who are called by My name put away
their pride and pray, and look for My face, and turn
from their sinful ways, then I will hear from heaven.
I will forgive their sin, and will heal their land."
2 CHRONICLES 7:14

Date:

Dear God,

Today was:

☐ GOOD
☐ VERY GOOD
☐ BAD
☐ VERY BAD
☐ _____
(Fill in the blank)

Right now I am:

☐ HAPPY
☐ WORRIED
☐ SAD
☐ MAD
☐ _____
(Fill in the blank)

With You in my life, God, every day can be a VERY GOOD day!

It's important to look for good things every day. Here's a list of good things that happened today:

....

....

....

....

....

....

God, thank You for good things!

God, You give me blessings—BIG and small—every day. Here's a list of all the blessings I noticed today:

....

....

....

....

God, thank You for blessings!

God, I want You to know. . .

....

....

....

....

....

....

Please help me make tomorrow
a VERY GOOD day! Amen.
GOOD NIGHT, GOD!

> *Give all your worries to [God]
> because He cares for you.*
> 1 PETER 5:7

Dear God,

Today was:

☐ GOOD
☐ VERY GOOD
☐ BAD
☐ VERY BAD
☐ _____
(Fill in the blank)

Right now I am:

☐ HAPPY
☐ WORRIED
☐ SAD
☐ MAD
☐ _____
(Fill in the blank)

With You in my life, God, every day can be a VERY GOOD day!

It's important to look for good things every day. Here's a list of good things that happened today:

God, thank You for good things!

God, You give me blessings—BIG and small—every day.
Here's a list of all the blessings I noticed today:

....

....

....

....

God, thank You for blessings!

God, I want You to know. . .

....

....

....

....

....

....

Please help me make tomorrow
a VERY GOOD day! Amen.
GOOD NIGHT, GOD!

I remember Your name in the night,
O Lord, and I have kept Your Law.
PSALM 119:55

Date:

Dear God,

Today was:

☐ GOOD
☐ VERY GOOD
☐ BAD
☐ VERY BAD
☐ _____
     (Fill in the blank)

Right now I am:

☐ HAPPY
☐ WORRIED
☐ SAD
☐ MAD
☐ _____
     (Fill in the blank)

With You in my life, God, every day can be a VERY GOOD day!

It's important to look for good things every day. Here's a list of good things that happened today:

....

....

....

....

....

....

God, thank You for good things!

God, You give me blessings—BIG and small—every day. Here's a list of all the blessings I noticed today:

....

....

....

....

God, thank You for blessings!

God, I want You to know. . .

....

....

....

....

....

....

Please help me make tomorrow a VERY GOOD day! Amen.

GOOD NIGHT, GOD!

You will not be afraid when you lie down. When you lie down, your sleep will be sweet.
PROVERBS 3:24

Date:

Dear God,

Today was:

☐ GOOD
☐ VERY GOOD
☐ BAD
☐ VERY BAD
☐ _____
(Fill in the blank)

Right now I am:

☐ HAPPY
☐ WORRIED
☐ SAD
☐ MAD
☐ _____
(Fill in the blank)

With You in my life, God, every day can be a VERY GOOD day!

It's important to look for good things every day. Here's a list of good things that happened today:

God, thank You for good things!

God, You give me blessings—BIG and small—every day.
Here's a list of all the blessings I noticed today:

....

....

....

....

God, thank You for blessings!

God, I want You to know. . .

....

....

....

....

....

Please help me make tomorrow
a VERY GOOD day! Amen.

GOOD NIGHT, GOD!

I prayed to the God of heaven.
NEHEMIAH 2:4

Date:

Dear God,

Today was:
- ☐ GOOD
- ☐ VERY GOOD
- ☐ BAD
- ☐ VERY BAD
- ☐ _____
  (Fill in the blank)

Right now I am:
- ☐ HAPPY
- ☐ WORRIED
- ☐ SAD
- ☐ MAD
- ☐ _____
  (Fill in the blank)

With You in my life, God, every day can be a VERY GOOD day!

It's important to look for good things every day. Here's a list of good things that happened today:

God, thank You for good things!

God, You give me blessings—BIG and small—every day. Here's a list of all the blessings I noticed today:

....

....

....

....

God, thank You for blessings!

God, I want You to know. . .

....

....

....

....

....

....

Please help me make tomorrow
a VERY GOOD day! Amen.
GOOD NIGHT, GOD!

*The Lord said, "I Myself will go
with you. I will give you rest."*
EXODUS 33:14

Date:

Dear God,

Today was:

- ☐ GOOD
- ☐ VERY GOOD
- ☐ BAD
- ☐ VERY BAD
- ☐ _____

(Fill in the blank)

Right now I am:

- ☐ HAPPY
- ☐ WORRIED
- ☐ SAD
- ☐ MAD
- ☐ _____

(Fill in the blank)

With You in my life, God, every day can be a VERY GOOD day!

It's important to look for good things every day. Here's a list of good things that happened today:

....

....

....

....

....

....

God, thank You for good things!

God, You give me blessings—BIG and small—every day.
Here's a list of all the blessings I noticed today:

....

....

....

....

God, thank You for blessings!

God, I want You to know. . .

....

....

....

....

....

....

Please help me make tomorrow
a VERY GOOD day! Amen.
GOOD NIGHT, GOD!

*He made the moon and stars to rule during the
night, for His loving-kindness lasts forever.*
PSALM 136:9

Dear God,

Today was:

☐ GOOD
☐ VERY GOOD
☐ BAD
☐ VERY BAD
☐ _____
(Fill in the blank)

Right now I am:

☐ HAPPY
☐ WORRIED
☐ SAD
☐ MAD
☐ _____
(Fill in the blank)

With You in my life, God, every day can be a VERY GOOD day!

It's important to look for good things every day. Here's a list of good things that happened today:

God, thank You for good things!

God, You give me blessings—BIG and small—every day.
Here's a list of all the blessings I noticed today:

....

....

....

....

God, thank You for blessings!

God, I want You to know. . .

....

....

....

....

....

Please help me make tomorrow
a VERY GOOD day! Amen.

GOOD NIGHT, GOD!

"If you will look for God and pray to the
All-powerful, if you are pure and right
and good, for sure He will help you."
JOB 8:5-6

Dear God,

Today was:

☐ GOOD
☐ VERY GOOD
☐ BAD
☐ VERY BAD
☐ _____
(Fill in the blank)

Right now I am:

☐ HAPPY
☐ WORRIED
☐ SAD
☐ MAD
☐ _____
(Fill in the blank)

With You in my life, God, every day can be a VERY GOOD day!

It's important to look for good things every day. Here's a list of good things that happened today:

God, thank You for good things!

God, You give me blessings—BIG and small—every day.
Here's a list of all the blessings I noticed today:

....

....

....

....

God, thank You for blessings!

God, I want You to know. . .

....

....

....

....

....

....

Please help me make tomorrow
a VERY GOOD day! Amen.
GOOD NIGHT, GOD!

Hear my prayer, O Lord. Listen when I ask for help.
Answer me because You are faithful and right.
PSALM 143:1

Date:

Dear God,

Today was:

☐ GOOD
☐ VERY GOOD
☐ BAD
☐ VERY BAD
☐ _____
(Fill in the blank)

Right now I am:

☐ HAPPY
☐ WORRIED
☐ SAD
☐ MAD
☐ _____
(Fill in the blank)

With You in my life, God, every day can be a VERY GOOD day!

It's important to look for good things every day. Here's a list of good things that happened today:

....

....

....

....

....

....

God, thank You for good things!

God, You give me blessings—BIG and small—every day.
Here's a list of all the blessings I noticed today:

....

....

....

....

God, thank You for blessings!

God, I want You to know. . .

....

....

....

....

....

Please help me make tomorrow
a VERY GOOD day! Amen.

GOOD NIGHT, GOD!

*When I look up and think about Your heavens,
the work of Your fingers, the moon and the
stars, which You have set in their place. . .*
PSALM 8:3

Date:

Dear God,

Today was:

☐ GOOD
☐ VERY GOOD
☐ BAD
☐ VERY BAD
☐ _____
(Fill in the blank)

Right now I am:

☐ HAPPY
☐ WORRIED
☐ SAD
☐ MAD
☐ _____
(Fill in the blank)

With You in my life, God, every day can be a VERY GOOD day!

It's important to look for good things every day. Here's a list of good things that happened today:

God, thank You for good things!

God, You give me blessings—BIG and small—every day. Here's a list of all the blessings I noticed today:

....

....

....

....

God, thank You for blessings!

God, I want You to know. . .

....

....

....

....

....

Please help me make tomorrow
a VERY GOOD day! Amen.
GOOD NIGHT, GOD!

*Let us go with complete trust to the throne of
God. We will receive His loving-kindness and have
His loving-favor to help us whenever we need it.*
HEBREWS 4:16

Date: _____

Dear God,

Today was:

☐ GOOD
☐ VERY GOOD
☐ BAD
☐ VERY BAD
☐ _____
(Fill in the blank)

Right now I am:

☐ HAPPY
☐ WORRIED
☐ SAD
☐ MAD
☐ _____
(Fill in the blank)

With You in my life, God, every day can be a VERY GOOD day!

It's important to look for good things every day.
Here's a list of good things that happened today:

....
....
....
....
....
....
....

God, thank You for good things!

God, You give me blessings—BIG and small—every day. Here's a list of all the blessings I noticed today:

....

....

....

....

God, thank You for blessings!

God, I want You to know. . .

....

....

....

....

....

....

Please help me make tomorrow
a VERY GOOD day! Amen.
GOOD NIGHT, GOD!

Praise Him, sun and moon!
Praise Him, all you shining stars!
PSALM 148:3

Date: _____

Dear God,

Today was:
- ☐ GOOD
- ☐ VERY GOOD
- ☐ BAD
- ☐ VERY BAD
- ☐ _____

(Fill in the blank)

Right now I am:
- ☐ HAPPY
- ☐ WORRIED
- ☐ SAD
- ☐ MAD
- ☐ _____

(Fill in the blank)

With You in my life, God, every day can be a VERY GOOD day!

It's important to look for good things every day. Here's a list of good things that happened today:

....

....

....

....

....

....

God, thank You for good things!

God, You give me blessings—BIG and small—every day.
Here's a list of all the blessings I noticed today:

....

....

....

....

God, thank You for blessings!

God, I want You to know. . .

....

....

....

....

....

Please help me make tomorrow
a VERY GOOD day! Amen.
GOOD NIGHT, GOD!

"Those who are wise will shine like the
bright heavens. And those who lead many
to do what is right and good will shine
like the stars forever and ever."
DANIEL 12:3

Date: _____

Dear God,

Today was:

☐ GOOD
☐ VERY GOOD
☐ BAD
☐ VERY BAD
☐ _____
(Fill in the blank)

Right now I am:

☐ HAPPY
☐ WORRIED
☐ SAD
☐ MAD
☐ _____
(Fill in the blank)

With You in my life, God, every day can be a VERY GOOD day!

It's important to look for good things every day. Here's a list of good things that happened today:

....

....

....

....

....

....

God, thank You for good things!

God, You give me blessings—BIG and small—every day.
Here's a list of all the blessings I noticed today:

....

....

....

....

God, thank You for blessings!

God, I want You to know. . .

....

....

....

....

....

Please help me make tomorrow
a VERY GOOD day! Amen.
GOOD NIGHT, GOD!

*You make my lamp bright. The Lord
my God lights my darkness.*
PSALM 18:28

Date:

Dear God,

Today was:
- ☐ GOOD
- ☐ VERY GOOD
- ☐ BAD
- ☐ VERY BAD
- ☐ _____
  (Fill in the blank)

Right now I am:
- ☐ HAPPY
- ☐ WORRIED
- ☐ SAD
- ☐ MAD
- ☐ _____
  (Fill in the blank)

With You in my life, God, every day can be a VERY GOOD day!

It's important to look for good things every day. Here's a list of good things that happened today:

God, thank You for good things!

God, You give me blessings—BIG and small—every day. Here's a list of all the blessings I noticed today:

....

....

....

....

God, thank You for blessings!

God, I want You to know. . .

....

....

....

....

....

Please help me make tomorrow
a VERY GOOD day! Amen.
GOOD NIGHT, GOD!

"If your whole body is full of light,
with no dark part, then it will shine.
It will be as a lamp that gives light."
LUKE 11:36

Date:

Dear God,

Today was:
- ☐ GOOD
- ☐ VERY GOOD
- ☐ BAD
- ☐ VERY BAD
- ☐ _____

(Fill in the blank)

Right now I am:
- ☐ HAPPY
- ☐ WORRIED
- ☐ SAD
- ☐ MAD
- ☐ _____

(Fill in the blank)

With You in my life, God, every day can be a VERY GOOD day!

It's important to look for good things every day. Here's a list of good things that happened today:

....

....

....

....

....

....

....

God, thank You for good things!

God, You give me blessings—BIG and small—every day. Here's a list of all the blessings I noticed today:

....

....

....

....

God, thank You for blessings!

God, I want You to know. . .

....

....

....

....

....

....

Please help me make tomorrow
a VERY GOOD day! Amen.
GOOD NIGHT, GOD!

> [Jesus said,] "I am the Light of the world.
> Anyone who follows Me will not walk in
> darkness. He will have the Light of Life."
> JOHN 8:12

Date:

Dear God,

Today was:

☐ GOOD
☐ VERY GOOD
☐ BAD
☐ VERY BAD
☐ _____
(Fill in the blank)

Right now I am:

☐ HAPPY
☐ WORRIED
☐ SAD
☐ MAD
☐ _____
(Fill in the blank)

With You in my life, God, every day can be a VERY GOOD day!

It's important to look for good things every day. Here's a list of good things that happened today:

God, thank You for good things!

God, You give me blessings—BIG and small—every day.
Here's a list of all the blessings I noticed today:

....

....

....

....

God, thank You for blessings!

God, I want You to know. . .

....

....

....

....

....

....

Please help me make tomorrow
a VERY GOOD day! Amen.
GOOD NIGHT, GOD!

The Lord is my light and the One Who saves me.
Whom should I fear? The Lord is the strength
of my life. Of whom should I be afraid?
PSALM 27:1

Date:

Dear God,

Today was:
- ☐ GOOD
- ☐ VERY GOOD
- ☐ BAD
- ☐ VERY BAD
- ☐ _____

(Fill in the blank)

Right now I am:
- ☐ HAPPY
- ☐ WORRIED
- ☐ SAD
- ☐ MAD
- ☐ _____

(Fill in the blank)

With You in my life, God, every day can be a VERY GOOD day!

It's important to look for good things every day. Here's a list of good things that happened today:

....

....

....

....

....

....

God, thank You for good things!

God, You give me blessings—BIG and small—every day.
Here's a list of all the blessings I noticed today:

....

....

....

....

God, thank You for blessings!

God, I want You to know. . .

....

....

....

....

....

Please help me make tomorrow
a VERY GOOD day! Amen.
GOOD NIGHT, GOD!

*May my prayer be like special perfume before
You. May the lifting up of my hands be like the
evening gift given on the altar in worship.*
PSALM 141:2

Date: _____

Dear God,

Today was:
- ☐ GOOD
- ☐ VERY GOOD
- ☐ BAD
- ☐ VERY BAD
- ☐ _____

(Fill in the blank)

Right now I am:
- ☐ HAPPY
- ☐ WORRIED
- ☐ SAD
- ☐ MAD
- ☐ _____

(Fill in the blank)

With You in my life, God, every day can be a VERY GOOD day!

It's important to look for good things every day. Here's a list of good things that happened today:

....

....

....

....

....

....

....

God, thank You for good things!

God, You give me blessings—BIG and small—every day. Here's a list of all the blessings I noticed today:

....

....

....

....

《《 God, thank You for blessings!

God, I want You to know. . .

....

....

....

....

....

....

Please help me make tomorrow
a VERY GOOD day! Amen.
GOOD NIGHT, GOD!

*May honor and thanks be given to the
Lord, because He has heard my prayer.*
PSALM 28:6

Date:

Dear God,

Today was:

☐ GOOD
☐ VERY GOOD
☐ BAD
☐ VERY BAD
☐ _____
(Fill in the blank)

Right now I am:

☐ HAPPY
☐ WORRIED
☐ SAD
☐ MAD
☐ _____
(Fill in the blank)

With You in my life, God, every day can be a VERY GOOD day!

It's important to look for good things every day. Here's a list of good things that happened today:

God, thank You for good things!

God, You give me blessings—BIG and small—every day.
Here's a list of all the blessings I noticed today:

....

....

....

God, thank You for blessings!

God, I want You to know. . .

....

....

....

....

....

....

Please help me make tomorrow
a VERY GOOD day! Amen.
GOOD NIGHT, GOD!

I lift up my soul to You, O Lord.
PSALM 25:1

Date:

Dear God,

Today was:

☐ GOOD
☐ VERY GOOD
☐ BAD
☐ VERY BAD
☐ _____
(Fill in the blank)

Right now I am:

☐ HAPPY
☐ WORRIED
☐ SAD
☐ MAD
☐ _____
(Fill in the blank)

With You in my life, God, every day can be a VERY GOOD day!

It's important to look for good things every day.
Here's a list of good things that happened today:

God, thank You for good things!

God, You give me blessings—BIG and small—every day.
Here's a list of all the blessings I noticed today:

....

....

....

God, thank You for blessings!

God, I want You to know. . .

....

....

....

....

....

Please help me make tomorrow
a VERY GOOD day! Amen.
GOOD NIGHT, GOD!

*Answer me when I call, O my God Who is right
and good! You have made a way for me when I
needed help. Be kind to me, and hear my prayer.*
PSALM 4:1

Date: _____

Dear God,

Today was:
- ☐ GOOD
- ☐ VERY GOOD
- ☐ BAD
- ☐ VERY BAD
- ☐ _____

(Fill in the blank)

Right now I am:
- ☐ HAPPY
- ☐ WORRIED
- ☐ SAD
- ☐ MAD
- ☐ _____

(Fill in the blank)

With You in my life, God, every day can be a VERY GOOD day!

It's important to look for good things every day. Here's a list of good things that happened today:

....

....

....

....

....

....

....

God, thank You for good things!

God, You give me blessings—BIG and small—every day. Here's a list of all the blessings I noticed today:

....

....

....

....

God, thank You for blessings!

God, I want You to know. . .

....

....

....

....

....

....

Please help me make tomorrow
a VERY GOOD day! Amen.
GOOD NIGHT, GOD!

"The Lord your God gives you rest."
JOSHUA 1:13

Date:

Dear God,

Today was:

☐ GOOD
☐ VERY GOOD
☐ BAD
☐ VERY BAD
☐ _____
(Fill in the blank)

Right now I am:

☐ HAPPY
☐ WORRIED
☐ SAD
☐ MAD
☐ _____
(Fill in the blank)

With You in my life, God, every day can be a VERY GOOD day!

It's important to look for good things every day.
Here's a list of good things that happened today:

God, thank You for good things!

God, You give me blessings—BIG and small—every day.
Here's a list of all the blessings I noticed today:

....

....

....

....

God, thank You for blessings!

God, I want You to know. . .

....

....

....

....

....

....

Please help me make tomorrow
a VERY GOOD day! Amen.
GOOD NIGHT, GOD!

*Listen to my prayer, O God. Do not
hide Yourself from what I ask.*
PSALM 55:1

Date:

Dear God,

Today was:

☐ GOOD
☐ VERY GOOD
☐ BAD
☐ VERY BAD
☐ _____
(Fill in the blank)

Right now I am:

☐ HAPPY
☐ WORRIED
☐ SAD
☐ MAD
☐ _____
(Fill in the blank)

With You in my life, God, every day can be a VERY GOOD day!

It's important to look for good things every day. Here's a list of good things that happened today:

God, thank You for good things!

God, You give me blessings—BIG and small—every day. Here's a list of all the blessings I noticed today:

....

....

....

....

God, thank You for blessings!

God, I want You to know. . .

....

....

....

....

....

....

Please help me make tomorrow a VERY GOOD day! Amen.

GOOD NIGHT, GOD!

The Lord made the stars of Pleiades and Orion. He changes darkness into morning, and turns day into night.
AMOS 5:8

Date: _____

Dear God,

Today was:

☐ GOOD
☐ VERY GOOD
☐ BAD
☐ VERY BAD
☐ _____
(Fill in the blank)

Right now I am:

☐ HAPPY
☐ WORRIED
☐ SAD
☐ MAD
☐ _____
(Fill in the blank)

With You in my life, God, every day can be a VERY GOOD day!

It's important to look for good things every day. Here's a list of good things that happened today:

....

....

....

....

....

....

....

God, thank You for good things!

God, You give me blessings—BIG and small—every day.
Here's a list of all the blessings I noticed today:

....

....

....

God, thank You for blessings!

God, I want You to know. . .

....

....

....

....

....

....

Please help me make tomorrow
a VERY GOOD day! Amen.

GOOD NIGHT, GOD!

*I love the Lord, because He hears
my voice and my prayers.*
PSALM 116:1

Date: _____

Dear God,

Today was:

- ☐ GOOD
- ☐ VERY GOOD
- ☐ BAD
- ☐ VERY BAD
- ☐ _____

(Fill in the blank)

Right now I am:

- ☐ HAPPY
- ☐ WORRIED
- ☐ SAD
- ☐ MAD
- ☐ _____

(Fill in the blank)

With You in my life, God, every day can be a VERY GOOD day!

It's important to look for good things every day. Here's a list of good things that happened today:

....

....

....

....

....

....

....

God, thank You for good things!

God, You give me blessings—BIG and small—every day. Here's a list of all the blessings I noticed today:

....

....

....

....

God, thank You for blessings!

God, I want You to know. . .

....

....

....

....

....

Please help me make tomorrow
a VERY GOOD day! Amen.
GOOD NIGHT, GOD!

> "I am glad and my tongue is full
> of joy. My body rests in hope."
> ACTS 2:26

Date: _____

Dear God,

Today was:
- ☐ GOOD
- ☐ VERY GOOD
- ☐ BAD
- ☐ VERY BAD
- ☐ _____
  (Fill in the blank)

Right now I am:
- ☐ HAPPY
- ☐ WORRIED
- ☐ SAD
- ☐ MAD
- ☐ _____
  (Fill in the blank)

With You in my life, God, every day can be a VERY GOOD day!

It's important to look for good things every day. Here's a list of good things that happened today:

....

....

....

....

....

....

God, thank You for good things!

God, You give me blessings—BIG and small—every day.
Here's a list of all the blessings I noticed today:

....

....

....

....

God, thank You for blessings!

God, I want You to know. . .

....

....

....

....

....

....

Please help me make tomorrow
a VERY GOOD day! Amen.
GOOD NIGHT, GOD!

*Do not let anything
stop you from praying.*
ROMANS 12:12

Dear God,

Today was:

☐ GOOD
☐ VERY GOOD
☐ BAD
☐ VERY BAD
☐ _____
(Fill in the blank)

Right now I am:

☐ HAPPY
☐ WORRIED
☐ SAD
☐ MAD
☐ _____
(Fill in the blank)

With You in my life, God, every day can be a VERY GOOD day!

It's important to look for good things every day. Here's a list of good things that happened today:

God, thank You for good things!

God, You give me blessings—BIG and small—every day.
Here's a list of all the blessings I noticed today:

....

....

....

God, thank You for blessings!

God, I want You to know. . .

....

....

....

....

....

....

Please help me make tomorrow
a VERY GOOD day! Amen.
GOOD NIGHT, GOD!

*"Respect and give thanks for those who
try to bring bad to you. Pray for those
who make it very hard for you."*
LUKE 6:28

Date: _____

Dear God,

Today was:
- ☐ GOOD
- ☐ VERY GOOD
- ☐ BAD
- ☐ VERY BAD
- ☐ _____

(Fill in the blank)

Right now I am:
- ☐ HAPPY
- ☐ WORRIED
- ☐ SAD
- ☐ MAD
- ☐ _____

(Fill in the blank)

With You in my life, God, every day can be a VERY GOOD day!

It's important to look for good things every day. Here's a list of good things that happened today:

....

....

....

....

....

....

God, thank You for good things!

God, You give me blessings—BIG and small—every day. Here's a list of all the blessings I noticed today:

....

....

....

....

God, thank You for blessings!

God, I want You to know. . .

....

....

....

....

....

Please help me make tomorrow
a VERY GOOD day! Amen.

GOOD NIGHT, GOD!

"Pray like this: 'Our Father in
heaven, Your name is holy.' "
MATTHEW 6:9

Date:

Dear God,

Today was:
- ☐ GOOD
- ☐ VERY GOOD
- ☐ BAD
- ☐ VERY BAD
- ☐ _____
  (Fill in the blank)

Right now I am:
- ☐ HAPPY
- ☐ WORRIED
- ☐ SAD
- ☐ MAD
- ☐ _____
  (Fill in the blank)

With You in my life, God, every day can be a VERY GOOD day!

It's important to look for good things every day. Here's a list of good things that happened today:

....

....

....

....

....

....

God, thank You for good things!

God, You give me blessings—BIG and small—every day.
Here's a list of all the blessings I noticed today:

....

....

....

....

God, thank You for blessings!

God, I want You to know. . .

....

....

....

....

....

....

Please help me make tomorrow
a VERY GOOD day! Amen.
GOOD NIGHT, GOD!

"The Lord my God has given me rest on every side.
There is no trouble or anything bad happening."
1 KINGS 5:4

Date: _____

Dear God,

Today was:

☐ GOOD
☐ VERY GOOD
☐ BAD
☐ VERY BAD
☐ _____
(Fill in the blank)

Right now I am:

☐ HAPPY
☐ WORRIED
☐ SAD
☐ MAD
☐ _____
(Fill in the blank)

With You in my life, God, every day can be a VERY GOOD day!

It's important to look for good things every day. Here's a list of good things that happened today:

....

....

....

....

....

....

God, thank You for good things!

God, You give me blessings—BIG and small—every day.
Here's a list of all the blessings I noticed today:

....

....

....

....

God, thank You for blessings!

God, I want You to know. . .

....

....

....

....

....

Please help me make tomorrow
a VERY GOOD day! Amen.
GOOD NIGHT, GOD!

Give thanks to the Lord, for He is good.
His loving-kindness lasts forever.
PSALM 118:1

Dear God,

Today was:
- [ ] GOOD
- [ ] VERY GOOD
- [ ] BAD
- [ ] VERY BAD
- [ ] _____
  (Fill in the blank)

Right now I am:
- [ ] HAPPY
- [ ] WORRIED
- [ ] SAD
- [ ] MAD
- [ ] _____
  (Fill in the blank)

With You in my life, God, every day can be a VERY GOOD day!

It's important to look for good things every day. Here's a list of good things that happened today:

....

....

....

....

....

....

God, thank You for good things!

God, You give me blessings—BIG and small—every day.
Here's a list of all the blessings I noticed today:

....

....

....

....

God, thank You for blessings!

God, I want You to know. . .

....

....

....

....

....

Please help me make tomorrow
a VERY GOOD day! Amen.
GOOD NIGHT, GOD!

[The Lord] hears the prayer
of those who are right with Him.
PROVERBS 15:29

Dear God,

Today was:

☐ GOOD
☐ VERY GOOD
☐ BAD
☐ VERY BAD
☐ _____
(Fill in the blank)

Right now I am:

☐ HAPPY
☐ WORRIED
☐ SAD
☐ MAD
☐ _____
(Fill in the blank)

With You in my life, God, every day can be a VERY GOOD day!

It's important to look for good things every day. Here's a list of good things that happened today:

God, thank You for good things!

God, You give me blessings—BIG and small—every day. Here's a list of all the blessings I noticed today:

....

....

....

....

God, thank You for blessings!

God, I want You to know. . .

....

....

....

....

....

....

Please help me make tomorrow
a VERY GOOD day! Amen.
GOOD NIGHT, GOD!

*Heal me, O Lord, and I will be healed. Save me
and I will be saved. For You are my praise.*
JEREMIAH 17:14

Date:

Dear God,

Today was:
- ☐ GOOD
- ☐ VERY GOOD
- ☐ BAD
- ☐ VERY BAD
- ☐ _____

(Fill in the blank)

Right now I am:
- ☐ HAPPY
- ☐ WORRIED
- ☐ SAD
- ☐ MAD
- ☐ _____

(Fill in the blank)

With You in my life, God, every day can be a VERY GOOD day!

It's important to look for good things every day. Here's a list of good things that happened today:

....

....

....

....

....

....

God, thank You for good things!

God, You give me blessings—BIG and small—every day. Here's a list of all the blessings I noticed today:

....

....

....

....

God, thank You for blessings!

God, I want You to know. . .

....

....

....

....

....

....

Please help me make tomorrow
a VERY GOOD day! Amen.
GOOD NIGHT, GOD!

> *"Everyone must pray to
> God with all [their] heart."*
> JONAH 3:8

Dear God,

Today was:

☐ GOOD
☐ VERY GOOD
☐ BAD
☐ VERY BAD
☐ _____
(Fill in the blank)

Right now I am:

☐ HAPPY
☐ WORRIED
☐ SAD
☐ MAD
☐ _____
(Fill in the blank)

With You in my life, God, every day can be a VERY GOOD day!

It's important to look for good things every day. Here's a list of good things that happened today:

....

....

....

....

....

....

....

God, thank You for good things!

God, You give me blessings—BIG and small—every day.
Here's a list of all the blessings I noticed today:

....

....

....

....

God, thank You for blessings!

God, I want You to know. . .

....

....

....

....

....

Please help me make tomorrow
a VERY GOOD day! Amen.
GOOD NIGHT, GOD!

*"I say to you, whatever you ask for
when you pray, have faith that you
will receive it. Then you will get it."*
MARK 11:24

Date: _____

Dear God,

Today was:
- ☐ GOOD
- ☐ VERY GOOD
- ☐ BAD
- ☐ VERY BAD
- ☐ _____
  (Fill in the blank)

Right now I am:
- ☐ HAPPY
- ☐ WORRIED
- ☐ SAD
- ☐ MAD
- ☐ _____
  (Fill in the blank)

With You in my life, God, every day can be a VERY GOOD day!

It's important to look for good things every day. Here's a list of good things that happened today:

....

....

....

....

....

....

God, thank You for good things!

God, You give me blessings—BIG and small—every day. Here's a list of all the blessings I noticed today:

....

....

....

....

God, thank You for blessings!

God, I want You to know. . .

....

....

....

....

....

Please help me make tomorrow
a VERY GOOD day! Amen.
GOOD NIGHT, GOD!

Is anyone among you suffering?
He should pray. Is anyone happy?
He should sing songs of thanks to God.
JAMES 5:13

Date:

Dear God,

Today was:
- ☐ GOOD
- ☐ VERY GOOD
- ☐ BAD
- ☐ VERY BAD
- ☐ _____

(Fill in the blank)

Right now I am:
- ☐ HAPPY
- ☐ WORRIED
- ☐ SAD
- ☐ MAD
- ☐ _____

(Fill in the blank)

With You in my life, God, every day can be a VERY GOOD day!

It's important to look for good things every day. Here's a list of good things that happened today:

....

....

....

....

....

....

God, thank You for good things!

God, You give me blessings—BIG and small—every day.
Here's a list of all the blessings I noticed today:

....

....

....

....

God, thank You for blessings!

God, I want You to know. . .

....

....

....

....

....

....

Please help me make tomorrow
a VERY GOOD day! Amen.
GOOD NIGHT, GOD!

*I cried out to You, O Lord. I said,
"You are my safe place."*
PSALM 142:5

Date:

Dear God,

Today was:
- ☐ GOOD
- ☐ VERY GOOD
- ☐ BAD
- ☐ VERY BAD
- ☐ _____
  (Fill in the blank)

Right now I am:
- ☐ HAPPY
- ☐ WORRIED
- ☐ SAD
- ☐ MAD
- ☐ _____
  (Fill in the blank)

With You in my life, God, every day can be a VERY GOOD day!

It's important to look for good things every day. Here's a list of good things that happened today:

....

....

....

....

....

....

....

God, thank You for good things!

God, You give me blessings—BIG and small—every day. Here's a list of all the blessings I noticed today:

....

....

....

....

God, thank You for blessings!

God, I want You to know. . .

....

....

....

....

....

Please help me make tomorrow a VERY GOOD day! Amen.
GOOD NIGHT, GOD!

"When you stand to pray, if you have anything against anyone, forgive him. Then your Father in heaven will forgive your sins also."
MARK 11:25

Date: _____

Dear God,

Today was:
- ☐ GOOD
- ☐ VERY GOOD
- ☐ BAD
- ☐ VERY BAD
- ☐ _____
  (Fill in the blank)

Right now I am:
- ☐ HAPPY
- ☐ WORRIED
- ☐ SAD
- ☐ MAD
- ☐ _____
  (Fill in the blank)

With You in my life, God, every day can be a VERY GOOD day!

It's important to look for good things every day. Here's a list of good things that happened today:

....

....

....

....

....

....

....

God, thank You for good things!

God, You give me blessings—BIG and small—every day.
Here's a list of all the blessings I noticed today:

....

....

....

....

God, thank You for blessings!

God, I want You to know. . .

....

....

....

....

....

....

Please help me make tomorrow
a VERY GOOD day! Amen.
GOOD NIGHT, GOD!

> "Now pray for God's favor,
> that He may be kind to us."
> MALACHI 1:9

Date:

Dear God,

Today was:
☐ GOOD
☐ VERY GOOD
☐ BAD
☐ VERY BAD
☐ _____
(Fill in the blank)

Right now I am:
☐ HAPPY
☐ WORRIED
☐ SAD
☐ MAD
☐ _____
(Fill in the blank)

With You in my life, God, every day can be a VERY GOOD day!

It's important to look for good things every day. Here's a list of good things that happened today:

God, thank You for good things!

God, You give me blessings—BIG and small—every day.
Here's a list of all the blessings I noticed today:

....

....

....

....

God, thank You for blessings!

God, I want You to know. . .

....

....

....

....

....

....

Please help me make tomorrow
a VERY GOOD day! Amen.
GOOD NIGHT, GOD!

The prayer of the faithful is [the Lord's] joy.
PROVERBS 15:8

Date:

Dear God,

Today was:
- ☐ GOOD
- ☐ VERY GOOD
- ☐ BAD
- ☐ VERY BAD
- ☐ _____
  (Fill in the blank)

Right now I am:
- ☐ HAPPY
- ☐ WORRIED
- ☐ SAD
- ☐ MAD
- ☐ _____
  (Fill in the blank)

With You in my life, God, every day can be a VERY GOOD day!

It's important to look for good things every day. Here's a list of good things that happened today:

God, thank You for good things!

God, You give me blessings—BIG and small—every day.
Here's a list of all the blessings I noticed today:

....

....

....

....

God, thank You for blessings!

God, I want You to know. . .

....

....

....

....

....

....

Please help me make tomorrow
a VERY GOOD day! Amen.
GOOD NIGHT, GOD!

My heart is glad. My soul is full of joy.
My body also will rest without fear.
PSALM 16:9

Date:

Dear God,

Today was:
- ☐ GOOD
- ☐ VERY GOOD
- ☐ BAD
- ☐ VERY BAD
- ☐ _____

(Fill in the blank)

Right now I am:
- ☐ HAPPY
- ☐ WORRIED
- ☐ SAD
- ☐ MAD
- ☐ _____

(Fill in the blank)

With You in my life, God, every day can be a VERY GOOD day!

It's important to look for good things every day. Here's a list of good things that happened today:

....

....

....

....

....

....

....

God, thank You for good things!

God, You give me blessings—BIG and small—every day.
Here's a list of all the blessings I noticed today:

....

....

....

....

God, thank You for blessings!

God, I want You to know. . .

....

....

....

....

....

....

Please help me make tomorrow
a VERY GOOD day! Amen.
GOOD NIGHT, GOD!

"I tell you this: If two of you agree on earth
about anything you pray for, it will be
done for you by My Father in heaven."
MATTHEW 18:19

Date: _____

Dear God,

Today was:
- ☐ GOOD
- ☐ VERY GOOD
- ☐ BAD
- ☐ VERY BAD
- ☐ _____

(Fill in the blank)

Right now I am:
- ☐ HAPPY
- ☐ WORRIED
- ☐ SAD
- ☐ MAD
- ☐ _____

(Fill in the blank)

With You in my life, God, every day can be a VERY GOOD day!

It's important to look for good things every day. Here's a list of good things that happened today:

....

....

....

....

....

....

....

God, thank You for good things!

God, You give me blessings—BIG and small—every day.
Here's a list of all the blessings I noticed today:

....

....

....

....

God, thank You for blessings!

God, I want You to know. . .

....

....

....

....

....

Please help me make tomorrow
a VERY GOOD day! Amen.
GOOD NIGHT, GOD!

Pray for the things that are needed.
You must watch and keep on praying.
Remember to pray for all Christians.
EPHESIANS 6:18

Date:

Dear God,

Today was:
- ☐ GOOD
- ☐ VERY GOOD
- ☐ BAD
- ☐ VERY BAD
- ☐ _____

(Fill in the blank)

Right now I am:
- ☐ HAPPY
- ☐ WORRIED
- ☐ SAD
- ☐ MAD
- ☐ _____

(Fill in the blank)

With You in my life, God, every day can be a VERY GOOD day!

It's important to look for good things every day. Here's a list of good things that happened today:

....

....

....

....

....

....

God, thank You for good things!

God, You give me blessings—BIG and small—every day.
Here's a list of all the blessings I noticed today:

....

....

....

....

God, thank You for blessings!

God, I want You to know. . .

....

....

....

....

....

....

Please help me make tomorrow
a VERY GOOD day! Amen.
GOOD NIGHT, GOD!

*"Thanks be to the Lord. He
has given rest to His people. . . .
He has done all that He promised."*
1 KINGS 8:56

Date: _____

Dear God,

Today was:
- ☐ GOOD
- ☐ VERY GOOD
- ☐ BAD
- ☐ VERY BAD
- ☐ _____

(Fill in the blank)

Right now I am:
- ☐ HAPPY
- ☐ WORRIED
- ☐ SAD
- ☐ MAD
- ☐ _____

(Fill in the blank)

With You in my life, God, every day can be a VERY GOOD day!

It's important to look for good things every day. Here's a list of good things that happened today:

....

....

....

....

....

....

....

God, thank You for good things!

God, You give me blessings—BIG and small—every day. Here's a list of all the blessings I noticed today:

_____

_____

_____

_____

God, thank You for blessings!

God, I want You to know. . .

_____

_____

_____

_____

_____

Please help me make tomorrow
a VERY GOOD day! Amen.
GOOD NIGHT, GOD!

*It is good to be near God. I have
made the Lord God my safe place.*
PSALM 73:28

Date:

Dear God,

Today was:

☐ GOOD
☐ VERY GOOD
☐ BAD
☐ VERY BAD
☐ _____
(Fill in the blank)

Right now I am:

☐ HAPPY
☐ WORRIED
☐ SAD
☐ MAD
☐ _____
(Fill in the blank)

With You in my life, God, every day can be a VERY GOOD day!

It's important to look for good things every day. Here's a list of good things that happened today:

....

....

....

....

....

....

God, thank You for good things!

God, You give me blessings—BIG and small—every day. Here's a list of all the blessings I noticed today:

....

....

....

....

God, thank You for blessings!

God, I want You to know. . .

....

....

....

....

....

Please help me make tomorrow
a VERY GOOD day! Amen.
GOOD NIGHT, GOD!

> *"Come to Me, all of you who work and
> have heavy loads. I will give you rest."*
> MATTHEW 11:28

Date: _____

Dear God,

Today was:
- ☐ GOOD
- ☐ VERY GOOD
- ☐ BAD
- ☐ VERY BAD
- ☐ _____
  (Fill in the blank)

Right now I am:
- ☐ HAPPY
- ☐ WORRIED
- ☐ SAD
- ☐ MAD
- ☐ _____
  (Fill in the blank)

With You in my life, God, every day can be a VERY GOOD day!

It's important to look for good things every day. Here's a list of good things that happened today:

....

....

....

....

....

....

God, thank You for good things!

God, You give me blessings—BIG and small—every day. Here's a list of all the blessings I noticed today:

....

....

....

....

God, thank You for blessings!

God, I want You to know. . .

....

....

....

....

....

....

Please help me make tomorrow
a VERY GOOD day! Amen.
GOOD NIGHT, GOD!

*I pray that you will see how great the
things are that He has promised to
those who belong to Him.*
EPHESIANS 1:18

Date:

Dear God,

Today was:
- ☐ GOOD
- ☐ VERY GOOD
- ☐ BAD
- ☐ VERY BAD
- ☐ _____
  (Fill in the blank)

Right now I am:
- ☐ HAPPY
- ☐ WORRIED
- ☐ SAD
- ☐ MAD
- ☐ _____
  (Fill in the blank)

With You in my life, God, every day can be a VERY GOOD day!

It's important to look for good things every day. Here's a list of good things that happened today:

....

....

....

....

....

....

God, thank You for good things!

God, You give me blessings—BIG and small—every day. Here's a list of all the blessings I noticed today:

....

....

....

....

God, thank You for blessings!

God, I want You to know. . .

....

....

....

....

....

....

Please help me make tomorrow a VERY GOOD day! Amen.
GOOD NIGHT, GOD!

I bow my knees and pray to the Father.
EPHESIANS 3:14

Dear God,

Today was:

☐ GOOD

☐ VERY GOOD

☐ BAD

☐ VERY BAD

☐ _____

(Fill in the blank)

Right now I am:

☐ HAPPY

☐ WORRIED

☐ SAD

☐ MAD

☐ _____

(Fill in the blank)

With You in my life, God, every day can be a VERY GOOD day!

It's important to look for good things every day. Here's a list of good things that happened today:

....

....

....

....

....

....

God, thank You for good things!

God, You give me blessings—BIG and small—every day.
Here's a list of all the blessings I noticed today:

....
....
....
....

God, thank You for blessings!

God, I want You to know. . .

....
....
....
....
....
....

Please help me make tomorrow
a VERY GOOD day! Amen.
GOOD NIGHT, GOD!

*"The Lord watches over those who are right
with Him. He hears their prayers."*
1 PETER 3:12

Date: _____

Dear God,

Today was:

☐ GOOD
☐ VERY GOOD
☐ BAD
☐ VERY BAD
☐ _____
(Fill in the blank)

Right now I am:

☐ HAPPY
☐ WORRIED
☐ SAD
☐ MAD
☐ _____
(Fill in the blank)

With You in my life, God, every day can be a VERY GOOD day!

It's important to look for good things every day. Here's a list of good things that happened today:

....

....

....

....

....

....

God, thank You for good things!

God, You give me blessings—BIG and small—every day. Here's a list of all the blessings I noticed today:

....

....

....

....

God, thank You for blessings!

God, I want You to know. . .

....

....

....

....

....

....

Please help me make tomorrow
a VERY GOOD day! Amen.
GOOD NIGHT, GOD!

*"When you pray, go into a room by yourself.
After you have shut the door, pray to your
Father Who is in secret. Then your Father
Who sees in secret will reward you."*
MATTHEW 6:6

Date: _____

Dear God,

Today was:

☐ GOOD
☐ VERY GOOD
☐ BAD
☐ VERY BAD
☐ _____
(Fill in the blank)

Right now I am:

☐ HAPPY
☐ WORRIED
☐ SAD
☐ MAD
☐ _____
(Fill in the blank)

With You in my life, God, every day can be a VERY GOOD day!

It's important to look for good things every day. Here's a list of good things that happened today:

....

....

....

....

....

....

God, thank You for good things!

God, You give me blessings—BIG and small—every day.
Here's a list of all the blessings I noticed today:

....

....

....

....

God, thank You for blessings!

God, I want You to know. . .

....

....

....

....

....

....

Please help me make tomorrow
a VERY GOOD day! Amen.
GOOD NIGHT, GOD!

Rest in the Lord and be willing to wait for Him.
PSALM 37:7

Date: _____

Dear God,

Today was:

☐ GOOD
☐ VERY GOOD
☐ BAD
☐ VERY BAD
☐ _____
(Fill in the blank)

Right now I am:

☐ HAPPY
☐ WORRIED
☐ SAD
☐ MAD
☐ _____
(Fill in the blank)

With You in my life, God, every day can be a VERY GOOD day!

It's important to look for good things every day. Here's a list of good things that happened today:

....

....

....

....

....

....

God, thank You for good things!

God, You give me blessings—BIG and small—every day. Here's a list of all the blessings I noticed today:

....

....

....

God, thank You for blessings!

God, I want You to know. . .

....

....

....

....

....

....

Please help me make tomorrow a VERY GOOD day! Amen.

GOOD NIGHT, GOD!

*"But the Lord is in His holy house.
Let all the earth be quiet before Him."*
HABAKKUK 2:20

Date:

Dear God,

Today was:
- ☐ GOOD
- ☐ VERY GOOD
- ☐ BAD
- ☐ VERY BAD
- ☐ _____

(Fill in the blank)

Right now I am:
- ☐ HAPPY
- ☐ WORRIED
- ☐ SAD
- ☐ MAD
- ☐ _____

(Fill in the blank)

With You in my life, God, every day can be a VERY GOOD day!

It's important to look for good things every day. Here's a list of good things that happened today:

....

....

....

....

....

....

....

God, thank You for good things!

God, You give me blessings—BIG and small—every day.
Here's a list of all the blessings I noticed today:

....

....

....

....

God, thank You for blessings!

God, I want You to know. . .

....

....

....

....

....

....

Please help me make tomorrow
a VERY GOOD day! Amen.
GOOD NIGHT, GOD!

"I will feed My sheep, and give
them rest," says the Lord God.
EZEKIEL 34:15

Date: _____

Dear God,

Today was:
- ☐ GOOD
- ☐ VERY GOOD
- ☐ BAD
- ☐ VERY BAD
- ☐ _____

(Fill in the blank)

Right now I am:
- ☐ HAPPY
- ☐ WORRIED
- ☐ SAD
- ☐ MAD
- ☐ _____

(Fill in the blank)

With You in my life, God, every day can be a VERY GOOD day!

It's important to look for good things every day. Here's a list of good things that happened today:

....

....

....

....

....

....

God, thank You for good things!

God, You give me blessings—BIG and small—every day. Here's a list of all the blessings I noticed today:

....

....

....

God, thank You for blessings!

God, I want You to know. . .

....

....

....

....

....

....

Please help me make tomorrow
a VERY GOOD day! Amen.
GOOD NIGHT, GOD!

*The Lord gives to His loved
ones even while they sleep.*
PSALM 127:2

Dear God,

Today was:

☐ GOOD
☐ VERY GOOD
☐ BAD
☐ VERY BAD
☐ _____
(Fill in the blank)

Right now I am:

☐ HAPPY
☐ WORRIED
☐ SAD
☐ MAD
☐ _____
(Fill in the blank)

With You in my life, God, every day can be a VERY GOOD day!

It's important to look for good things every day. Here's a list of good things that happened today:

....

....

....

....

....

....

God, thank You for good things!

God, You give me blessings—BIG and small—every day. Here's a list of all the blessings I noticed today:

....

....

....

....

God, thank You for blessings!

God, I want You to know. . .

....

....

....

....

....

....

Please help me make tomorrow
a VERY GOOD day! Amen.

GOOD NIGHT, GOD!

Be quiet and know that I am God.
I will be honored among the nations.
I will be honored in the earth.
PSALM 46:10

Dear God,

Today was:

☐ GOOD
☐ VERY GOOD
☐ BAD
☐ VERY BAD
☐ _____

(Fill in the blank)

Right now I am:

☐ HAPPY
☐ WORRIED
☐ SAD
☐ MAD
☐ _____

(Fill in the blank)

With You in my life, God, every day can be a VERY GOOD day!

It's important to look for good things every day. Here's a list of good things that happened today:

God, thank You for good things!

God, You give me blessings—BIG and small—every day.
Here's a list of all the blessings I noticed today:

....

....

....

....

God, thank You for blessings!

God, I want You to know. . .

....

....

....

....

....

....

Please help me make tomorrow
a VERY GOOD day! Amen.
GOOD NIGHT, GOD!

*My people will live in a place of peace,
in safe homes, and in quiet resting places.*
ISAIAH 32:18

Date:

Dear God,

Today was:

☐ GOOD
☐ VERY GOOD
☐ BAD
☐ VERY BAD
☐ _____

(Fill in the blank)

Right now I am:

☐ HAPPY
☐ WORRIED
☐ SAD
☐ MAD
☐ _____

(Fill in the blank)

With You in my life, God, every day can be a VERY GOOD day!

It's important to look for good things every day. Here's a list of good things that happened today:

God, thank You for good things!

God, You give me blessings—BIG and small—every day. Here's a list of all the blessings I noticed today:

....

....

....

....

God, thank You for blessings!

God, I want You to know. . .

....

....

....

....

....

....

Please help me make tomorrow
a VERY GOOD day! Amen.
GOOD NIGHT, GOD!

*It is good when you pray like this. It pleases
God Who is the One Who saves.*
1 TIMOTHY 2:3

Date:

Dear God,

Today was:
- ☐ GOOD
- ☐ VERY GOOD
- ☐ BAD
- ☐ VERY BAD
- ☐ _____
  (Fill in the blank)

Right now I am:
- ☐ HAPPY
- ☐ WORRIED
- ☐ SAD
- ☐ MAD
- ☐ _____
  (Fill in the blank)

With You in my life, God, every day can be a VERY GOOD day!

It's important to look for good things every day. Here's a list of good things that happened today:

....

....

....

....

....

....

....

God, thank You for good things!

God, You give me blessings—BIG and small—every day. Here's a list of all the blessings I noticed today:

....

....

....

God, thank You for blessings!

God, I want You to know. . .

....

....

....

....

....

....

Please help me make tomorrow a VERY GOOD day! Amen.
GOOD NIGHT, GOD!

Do not talk much about tomorrow, for you do not know what a day will bring.
PROVERBS 27:1

Dear God,

Today was:

☐ GOOD
☐ VERY GOOD
☐ BAD
☐ VERY BAD
☐ _____
(Fill in the blank)

Right now I am:

☐ HAPPY
☐ WORRIED
☐ SAD
☐ MAD
☐ _____
(Fill in the blank)

With You in my life, God, every day can be a VERY GOOD day!

It's important to look for good things every day. Here's a list of good things that happened today:

....

....

....

....

....

....

....

God, thank You for good things!

God, You give me blessings—BIG and small—every day.
Here's a list of all the blessings I noticed today:

....

....

....

....

God, thank You for blessings!

God, I want You to know. . .

....

....

....

....

....

....

Please help me make tomorrow
a VERY GOOD day! Amen.
GOOD NIGHT, GOD!

*We give thanks to the God and Father of our
Lord Jesus Christ. He is our Father Who shows us
loving-kindness and our God Who gives us comfort.*
2 CORINTHIANS 1:3

Date:

Dear God,

Today was:
- ☐ GOOD
- ☐ VERY GOOD
- ☐ BAD
- ☐ VERY BAD
- ☐ _____

(Fill in the blank)

Right now I am:
- ☐ HAPPY
- ☐ WORRIED
- ☐ SAD
- ☐ MAD
- ☐ _____

(Fill in the blank)

With You in my life, God, every day can be a VERY GOOD day!

It's important to look for good things every day. Here's a list of good things that happened today:

....

....

....

....

....

....

....

God, thank You for good things!

God, You give me blessings—BIG and small—every day.
Here's a list of all the blessings I noticed today:

....

....

....

....

God, thank You for blessings!

God, I want You to know. . .

....

....

....

....

....

Please help me make tomorrow
a VERY GOOD day! Amen.
GOOD NIGHT, GOD!

"Now the whole earth is at rest and quiet."
ISAIAH 14:7

Date: _____

Dear God,

Today was:
- ☐ GOOD
- ☐ VERY GOOD
- ☐ BAD
- ☐ VERY BAD
- ☐ _____

(Fill in the blank)

Right now I am:
- ☐ HAPPY
- ☐ WORRIED
- ☐ SAD
- ☐ MAD
- ☐ _____

(Fill in the blank)

With You in my life, God, every day can be a VERY GOOD day!

It's important to look for good things every day. Here's a list of good things that happened today:

....

....

....

....

....

....

....

God, thank You for good things!

God, You give me blessings—BIG and small—every day. Here's a list of all the blessings I noticed today:

....

....

....

....

God, thank You for blessings!

God, I want You to know. . .

....

....

....

....

....

....

Please help me make tomorrow
a VERY GOOD day! Amen.
GOOD NIGHT, GOD!

*Your Word is a lamp to my feet
and a light to my path.*
PSALM 119:105

Date:

Dear God,

Today was:
- ☐ GOOD
- ☐ VERY GOOD
- ☐ BAD
- ☐ VERY BAD
- ☐ _____

(Fill in the blank)

Right now I am:
- ☐ HAPPY
- ☐ WORRIED
- ☐ SAD
- ☐ MAD
- ☐ _____

(Fill in the blank)

With You in my life, God, every day can be a VERY GOOD day!

It's important to look for good things every day. Here's a list of good things that happened today:

God, thank You for good things!

God, You give me blessings—BIG and small—every day.
Here's a list of all the blessings I noticed today:

....
....
....
....

God, thank You for blessings!

God, I want You to know. . .

....
....
....
....
....
....

Please help me make tomorrow
a VERY GOOD day! Amen.
GOOD NIGHT, GOD!

Return to your rest, O my soul.
For the Lord has been good to you.
PSALM 116:7

Date:

Dear God,

Today was:
- ☐ GOOD
- ☐ VERY GOOD
- ☐ BAD
- ☐ VERY BAD
- ☐ _____

(Fill in the blank)

Right now I am:
- ☐ HAPPY
- ☐ WORRIED
- ☐ SAD
- ☐ MAD
- ☐ _____

(Fill in the blank)

With You in my life, God, every day can be a VERY GOOD day!

It's important to look for good things every day. Here's a list of good things that happened today:

....

....

....

....

....

....

God, thank You for good things!

God, You give me blessings—BIG and small—every day.
Here's a list of all the blessings I noticed today:

....

....

....

....

God, thank You for blessings!

God, I want You to know. . .

....

....

....

....

....

Please help me make tomorrow
a VERY GOOD day! Amen.
GOOD NIGHT, GOD!

*"For You are my lamp, O Lord. The
Lord gives light to my darkness."*
2 SAMUEL 22:29

Date: _____

Dear God,

Today was:

☐ GOOD
☐ VERY GOOD
☐ BAD
☐ VERY BAD
☐ _____
(Fill in the blank)

Right now I am:

☐ HAPPY
☐ WORRIED
☐ SAD
☐ MAD
☐ _____
(Fill in the blank)

With You in my life, God, every day can be a VERY GOOD day!

It's important to look for good things every day. Here's a list of good things that happened today:

....

....

....

....

....

....

....

God, thank You for good things!

God, You give me blessings—BIG and small—every day. Here's a list of all the blessings I noticed today:

....

....

....

....

God, thank You for blessings!

God, I want You to know. . .

....

....

....

....

....

....

Please help me make tomorrow
a VERY GOOD day! Amen.
GOOD NIGHT, GOD!

Never stop praying.
1 THESSALONIANS 5:17

Check Out These
Fantastically Fun Prayer Maps!

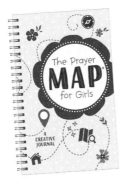 

The Prayer Map for Girls
978-1-68322-559-1

The Prayer Map for Boys
978-1-68322-558-4

These prayer journals are a fun and creative way to more fully experience the power of prayer. Each page guides you to write out thoughts, ideas, and lists. . .which then creates a specific "map" for you to follow as you talk to God. Each map includes a spot to record the date, so you can look back on your prayers and see how God has worked in your life. *The Prayer Map* will not only encourage you to spend time talking with God about the things that matter most. . .it will also help you build a healthy spiritual habit of continual prayer for life!

Spiral Bound / $7.99